Childhoods of the Presidents

John F. Kennedy

Childhoods
of the
Presidents

John Adams

George W. Bush

Bill Clinton

Ulysses S. Grant

Andrew Jackson

Thomas Jefferson

John F. Kennedy

Abraham Lincoln

James Madison

James Monroe

Ronald Reagan

Franklin D. Roosevelt

Theodore Roosevelt

Harry S. Truman

George Washington

Woodrow Wilson

John F. Kennedy

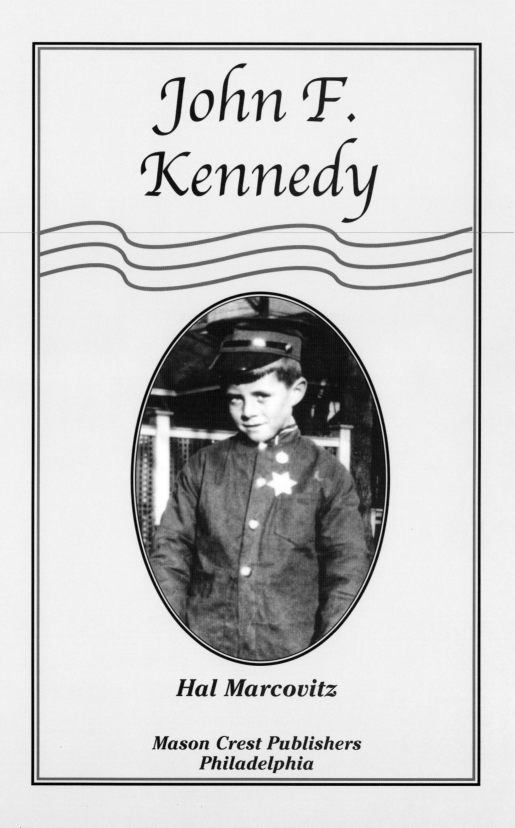

Hal Marcovitz

Mason Crest Publishers
Philadelphia

Produced by OTTN Publishing, Stockton, New Jersey

Mason Crest Publishers
370 Reed Road
Broomall, PA 19008
www.masoncrest.com

3 5 7 9 8 6 4 2

Library of Congress Cataloging-in-Publication Data

Marcovitz, Hal.
  John F. Kennedy / Hal Marcovitz.
    p.   cm.   (Childhood of the presidents)
  Summary: A biography of the thirty-fifth president of the United
States, focusing on his childhood and young adulthood.
  Includes bibliographical references (p.) and index.
    ISBN 1-59084-272-3 (hc.)
  1. Kennedy, John F. (John Fitzgerald), 1917-1963—Childhood and
youth—Juvenile literature. 2. Presidents—United States—
Biography—Juvenile literature. [1. Kennedy, John F. (John
Fitzgerald), 1917-1963—Childhood and youth. 2. Presidents.]
  I. Title. II. Series.
  E842.Z9 M37 2003
  973.922'092—dc21
  [B]   2002024442

Childhoods
of the
Presidents

Table of Contents

★★★★★★★★★★★★★★★★★

★ *Introduction* ★

Alexis de Tocqueville began his great work *Democracy in America* with a discourse on childhood. If we are to understand the prejudices, the habits and the passions that will rule a man's life, Tocqueville said, we must watch the baby in his mother's arms; we must see the first images that the world casts upon the mirror of his mind; we must hear the first words that awaken his sleeping powers of thought. "The entire man," he wrote, "is, so to speak, to be seen in the cradle of the child."

That is why these books on the childhoods of the American presidents are so much to the point. And, as our history shows, a great variety of childhoods can lead to the White House. The record confirms the ancient adage that every American boy, no matter how unpromising his beginnings, can aspire to the presidency. Soon, one hopes, the adage will be extended to include every American girl.

All our presidents thus far have been white males who, within the limits of their gender, reflect the diversity of American life. They were born in nineteen of our states; eight of the last thirteen presidents were born west of the Mississippi. Of all our presidents, Abraham Lincoln had the least promising childhood, yet he became our greatest president. Oddly enough, presidents who are children of privilege sometimes feel an obligation to reform society in order to give children of poverty a better break. And, with Lincoln the great exception, presidents who are children of poverty sometimes feel that there is no need to reform a society that has enabled them to rise from privation to the summit.

Does schooling make a difference? Harry S. Truman, the only twentieth-century president never to attend college, is generally accounted a near-great president. Actually nine— more than one fifth—of our presidents never went to college at all, including such luminaries as George Washington, Andrew Jackson and Grover Cleveland. But, Truman aside, all the non-college men held the highest office before the twentieth century, and, given the increasing complexity of life, a college education will unquestionably be a necessity in the twenty-first century.

Every reader of this book, girls included, has a right to aspire to the presidency. As you survey the childhoods of those who made it, try to figure out the qualities that brought them to the White House. I would suggest that among those qualities are ambition, determination, discipline, education— and luck.

—ARTHUR M. SCHLESINGER, JR.

Joseph Kennedy Sr. stands with his children, Joseph Jr. and John F. "Jack" Kennedy, who are on the running board of a Rolls Royce automobile.

Pals and *Playmates*

*J*oseph Kennedy Sr. had big plans for his son. The boy was smart, good-looking, athletic, and a natural leader with a wide, confident smile. Kennedy believed his son could accomplish whatever goal he set for the boy.

And Joe Kennedy set some lofty goals for his son. Election to the United States *House of Representatives* or even the *Senate* was not out of the question. In fact, Joe Kennedy dreamed that his eldest son, Joe Kennedy Jr., would one day be president.

It was an ambition shared by Joe Jr. While still very young, the boy developed an interest in politics and government. He often pestered his grandfather, John Francis Fitzgerald, for information about how to run for office. Fitzgerald, known as "Honey Fitz," was a former congressman and mayor of Boston, Massachusetts, as well as a longtime leader of the Democratic Party in his city.

Joe Kennedy Sr. liked to talk about current events at the dinner table and often posed questions to his children regarding the issues in the news. Joe Jr. was an enthusiastic participant at the dinner table conversations and enjoyed trading opinions with his father on national and world events.

Joe's younger brother John would participate in the dinner conversations as well. Two years younger than Joe, he was also thinner and not as athletic. He seemed as bright as Joe, although his grades in school were often just so-so. And while Joe was outgoing and at ease in front of others, John was shy and often withdrawn. Yet, John—who was called Jack by his parents—did his best to keep up with his older brother. In fact, the two boys were very competitive.

"Being brothers and less than two years apart in age had its advantages and its disadvantages," recalled the boys' mother, Rose Kennedy. "Generally, they were good pals and play-mates and shared all sorts of experiences and adventures together, including getting into mischief. But I suppose it was inevitable that they were also rivals."

The two boys fought constantly. The Kennedys loved to play sports. Joe enjoyed the games, but he was usually partic-ularly rough with his brother—jamming a football into his stomach during a game of touch football, for example, or throwing a baseball hard enough to sting Jack's hand.

While Jack rarely beat his brother at football or baseball, he found other ways to get even. Jack had a streak of mischief in him, and he often came up with schemes to annoy Joe.

Joe loved to eat and was especially fond of chocolate cake. One time, just as the cake was being served, Jack reached across the table, stole Joe's piece, and hurried out of the house. Joe ran after him but failed to catch his brother before Jack managed to stuff Joe's slice of cake into his mouth. To escape

Joe Jr. and Jack hold hands in this 1921 photograph. The two boys were very close, but also very competitive.

his brother, Jack ran down to a nearby dock and dove into the bay near the Kennedy house. Joe cornered him there, remaining on the dock while Jack treaded water in the bay. Finally, Jack tired and had to climb back onto the dock. Joe was waiting for him. He delivered a sound beating to his brother—punishment not only for stealing his piece of cake, but also for embarrassing him in front of the other members of the family.

Jack took a licking that day. But his mother recalled that at other times, the younger boy did manage to hold his own. "Joe Jr. was older, bigger, stronger, but Jack, frail though he was, could fight like fury when he had to," Rose said.

Although the two brothers competed and fought hard against each other, they were still very close. They could be counted on to support each other during difficult times. In 1936, when Jack was a teenager, he grew weak from hepatitis, a disease of the liver. Jack spent months in a hospital but was unable to regain his strength. The illness forced him to take a leave from school. Finally, his family decided that a few months in Arizona would help Jack regain his health. Joe Kennedy Sr. found Jack a job on the Jay Six cattle ranch near the Mexico border. Jack's job required him to keep the ranch's barbed wire in repair. This meant the boy had to take long horseback rides across the sprawling ranch.

Shortly after Jack left for the ranch job, Joe Jr. arrived home from college for the summer. He had just two months to enjoy himself away from his studies, but when he learned that his younger brother was on his way to Arizona to work on a ranch, Joe insisted on joining him.

When Joe arrived, he went to work as well, spending all day on horseback alongside Jack. Together the brothers

Jack and Joe Jr., wearing their navy uniforms, in one of the last photographs taken of the brothers together, 1942. On August 12, 1944, Joe was killed when the airplane he was flying exploded.

checked and, when necessary, repaired the wire along the boundaries of the 43,000-acre ranch. Soon, they were needed for other duties. John Speiden, the ranch owner, wanted to build *adobe* huts on the ranch and enlisted Jack and Joe for the job. Each day, Jack and Joe rose at dawn and worked under the broiling Arizona sun, lifting hundreds of adobe bricks to help build the huts. They slept in the bunkhouse with the other ranch hands. Speiden paid them each one dollar a day.

The hard work seemed to help Jack recover from the weakness caused by hepatitis. He regained his strength over the summer, and that fall he was able to carry on with his schoolwork. Joe returned to college that fall as well.

Five years later, Japanese warplanes attacked the Pearl Harbor naval base in Hawaii, pulling the United States into World War II. Jack and Joe had both enlisted in the U.S. Navy.

Jack became skipper of a PT boat—a small, fast boat armed with guns and *torpedoes*. He served in the waters of the Pacific, fighting the Japanese.

Joe became a navy pilot. At the controls of a bomber, he flew dozens of missions over Europe against Nazi Germany. Although he completed enough missions to return home, Joe turned down an opportunity to head back to the United States in May 1944. He decided instead to remain on combat duty until the end of the war. On August 12, 1944, Joe's plane exploded after leaving an airfield in England. Joe Kennedy Jr. was killed.

The Kennedys were devastated. Years later, though, Jack would fulfill all the political ambitions Joe Kennedy Sr. had set for his oldest son.

Five of the Kennedy children—Rosemary, Jack, Eunice, Joe Jr., and Kathleen—enjoy a dip in the ocean near the family home in Hyannis Port.

Hyannis Port

Hyannis Port can be found on Cape Cod—a 40-mile-long finger of land that curls east from mainland Massachusetts into the Atlantic Ocean. Hyannis Port, like other towns along the southern shore of the *cape*, enjoys a breathtaking view of Nantucket *Sound*—the area of ocean surrounded by the cape and the islands of Martha's Vineyard and Nantucket. Some of the richest families in America own homes in Hyannis Port and the other Cape Cod towns. The Kennedys are one of those families. In 1928, Joseph Kennedy Sr. bought a 17-room mansion in Hyannis Port.

The family also owned homes in Westchester, New York, and Palm Beach, Florida. But it was the mansion in Hyannis Port that would forever be identified as the Kennedy family home.

The mansion is perched atop a grassy hill that offers its residents a sweeping view of Nantucket Sound. Down below, the Kennedy children—there were eventually nine brothers and sisters—enjoyed sailing, waterskiing, and playing on their private beach. Back on land, the children made use of the tennis court on the property or played touch football on the lawn. Joe Sr. always made sure his children were involved in plenty of sports. He even hired a coach to lead the two oldest boys, Jack and Joe Jr., in *calisthenics* every morning.

What was life like at Hyannis Port? Rose Kennedy recalled "the bounce of the tennis balls, the splashings and belly flops and cannon balls in the ocean, the radios and phonographs, the cars revving up and backfiring, departing and arriving, the cries of welcome and farewell, the piano being tortured by someone learning to play, the yapping and barking of several involved dogs, the ringing of telephones and the maids' knocks on my door."

As children of one of the wealthiest men in America, Jack Kennedy and his brothers and sisters knew few hardships, but that certainly wasn't true of their ancestors. Jack's great-grandfather, Patrick Kennedy, was an *immigrant* from Ireland who arrived penniless in Boston in 1849. Patrick Kennedy came to America to escape starvation in Ireland, where the potato crop had failed. Between 1845 and 1849 more than a million Irish citizens died from starvation and disease. More than a million others left their country, many of them making their way to the United States.

Few of them had money when they arrived, and Patrick Kennedy was no exception. Kennedy and his young wife, Bridget, were forced to live in a squalid tenement in Boston. He found work as a dockhand and later as a barrel maker. He died at the age of 35, a victim of the disease *cholera*.

Patrick and Bridget Kennedy had three daughters and a son. The son, Patrick Joseph Kennedy, became a Boston busi-

The wedding of Joseph Kennedy and Rose Fitzgerald on October 7, 1914, was a major social event in Boston. Joe was president of a bank—a very prestigious position for a 26-year-old. Rose, as the daughter of Boston's former mayor, had been in the public eye for many years.

nessman, buying two *saloons* and a liquor-importing business. He was also the first Kennedy to enter Boston politics, serving three terms in the Massachusetts Senate. His son, Joseph Kennedy, was born in 1888.

Joe Kennedy was bright, hardworking, ambitious, and determined to make his fortune. He entered Harvard University near Boston at a time when few Irish Catholics were granted admission. Although there was a large Irish Catholic population in Boston at the time, they were often denied the best jobs and opportunities for education by the wealthy Protestants who ruled over Massachusetts society for generations. The wealthy and cultured Protestants were known as the "Boston Brahmins."

Still, Joe Kennedy's intelligence and drive overcame any barriers thrown up by the Brahmins. In 1913—a year after he graduated from Harvard—Kennedy became the youngest bank president in America. He extended his business to New York, where he became an influential Wall Street *financier*. Later, he would take control of movie studios in California.

Along the way he met and married Rose Fitzgerald, daughter of Boston's former mayor John Francis "Honey Fitz" Fitzgerald—a charming, witty, old-style politician who loved to tell a good joke. Joe Kennedy Jr. was born in 1915. The second son—John Fitzgerald Kennedy—arrived on May 29, 1917, while the family resided at 83 Beals Street in the Boston suburb of Brookline, Massachusetts.

Jack would be followed by seven brothers and sisters: Rosemary in 1918; Kathleen, who was called Kick by her brothers and sisters, in 1920; Eunice, in 1921; Patricia, in 1924; Robert, who was called Bobby, in 1925; Jean, in 1928; and, finally, Edward, who was called Teddy, in 1932.

"With Bobby's arrival I had had a child on the average of once every 18 months and by then had seven children, the eldest of whom was only a little more than 10 years old," Rose said. "I must say that even I, now that I

The Kennedys' second son was born at three o'clock on the afternoon of May 29, 1917. He was named after his mother's father, John Fitzgerald, the former mayor of Boston.

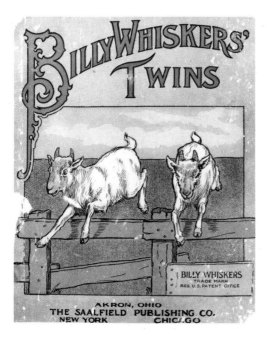

As a young boy, Jack Kennedy's favorite book was *Billy Whiskers*, a story about a billy goat who travels across the Pacific Ocean.

stop and do these calculations, find this arithmetic rather amazing, even though it didn't seem particularly unusual in the decade of 1915 to 1925. And, of course, Jean and Teddy were still to come."

As the Kennedy family kept growing, Joe Kennedy's success in business continued to rise as well. The Kennedys soon moved out of the Beals Street house into larger quarters. Eventually, Joe and Rose bought a large home in Westchester, an exclusive suburb of New York, so that Joe Kennedy could see to his business on Wall Street. He later bought the vacation homes in Hyannis Port and Palm Beach, where the family spent winters.

It was a big family full of energy and adventurous kids, but the Kennedys suffered through some trying times. Rosemary, the oldest daughter, consistently had trouble in school. Eventually, Joe and Rose learned that she was ***mentally***

Rose Kennedy kept track of her children's health on index cards, marking inoculations and illnesses with colored stickers. The cards were kept in this wooden box; Jack Kennedy's card is showing.

retarded and would need special care for the rest of her life. Today, schools and government agencies provide many services for mentally retarded individuals in the hopes that they can function in society. But in the 1920s not much was known about mental retardation. Eventually, the Kennedys sent Rosemary away to live in a Catholic convent in Wisconsin where she would be taken care of by nuns. Not until Jack Kennedy's presidential campaign in 1960 did the family admit to his sister's affliction.

Jack also gave his parents considerable cause for concern, mostly because of his health problems. He was thinner and less athletic than his older brother, but his health problems ran deeper than simply being unable to outrun or outfight Joe Jr.

"Almost all his life, it seemed, he had to do battle against misfortunes of health," wrote his mother.

Jack's first serious ailment occurred when he was three years old. He contracted scarlet fever, an infection accompanied by high fever, which often causes the skin to break out in a red rash. By the time he was eight years old, he had been through cases of whooping cough, measles, chicken pox, and German measles. He suffered from bronchitis and asthma, illnesses that make it difficult to breathe. At age 11, he felt sharp pains in his side, and was soon in surgery to have his *appendix* removed. He needed glasses to read, and he often had a sore back—an ailment he endured even as he helped build the adobe huts in Arizona while recovering from hepatitis.

"At least one-half the days he spent on this earth were days of intense physical pain," Bobby Kennedy later wrote. "He had scarlet fever when he was very young and serious back trouble when he was older. In between he had almost every other conceivable ailment. When we were growing up together we used to laugh about the great risk a mosquito took in biting Jack Kennedy—with some of his blood the mosquito was sure to die."

Despite his physical problems, Jack did his best to compete. He was forever trying to match his older brother's successes, but he never seemed to be able to keep up with Joe Jr. Joe Kennedy Sr. loved football and encouraged his sons to play. Joe Jr., who followed his father to Harvard, made the *varsity* football team. Jack went to Harvard, too. But he didn't make the varsity team.

His college friend Torby Macdonald recalled, "Jack couldn't have weighed more than 150 or 160. He was great on offense and could tackle well on defense, but as far as blocking and that sort of thing, where size mattered, he was under quite a handicap."

Jack and his sister Eunice are seated in the bow of a small boat, with Joe Jr. in the center and Rosemary and Kathleen in the stern. Jack grew to love the sea and became a very good sailor.

Plenty of Guts

*T*o fill their long idle hours at sea, whalers in the 1800s would take the bones or teeth of whales or the ivory from walrus tusks and polish them to a hard gloss. The whalers would carve them down with knives and then, using ink or *lampblack*, paint tiny images on them. This form of art is known as scrimshaw.

When he grew older, Jack Kennedy amassed a large collection of scrimshaw. His collection featured whales' teeth with images of sailing ships and harpooners, as well as portraits of historical figures, including American patriot Alexander Hamilton and kings of European nations. One whale tooth in the Kennedy collection features a drawing of the White House.

Spending his summers along the beaches of Hyannis Port, Jack Kennedy couldn't help but develop a love for the sea and water sports. Sailing became his passion. Many people on Cape Cod owned sailboats and *yachts* and enjoyed staging races across Nantucket Sound. When Jack Kennedy was 10 years old, he helped Joe Jr. sail the family boat *Rose Elizabeth* in a race across the sound. Not only were the boys declared the winners, but shortly after the race they dashed back out into the sound to rescue a racer who had fallen overboard. A reporter for the *Boston Post* witnessed the rescue, calling it "daring." Joe Jr. and Jack were now local heroes.

The other Kennedy children enjoyed sailing as well. Kick and Eunice were particularly good sailors. All the children were encouraged by their father to enter every race with the object of winning.

"Daddy was always very competitive," Eunice said. "The thing he always kept telling us was that coming in second was just no good."

The Kennedy children were so intensely competitive that during one sailboat race, when seven-year-old Teddy failed to follow Joe Jr.'s orders, the older brother grasped the little boy by the waist and tossed him overboard. Joe Jr. immediately realized what he had done and jumped overboard to retrieve his little brother. After the rescue, Joe Jr. still managed to place second in the race.

The Kennedys were competitive in their games on land, too. Touch football was a favorite sport on the two-acre lawn in front of the Hyannis Port home. Even though no tackling was allowed, the games often included a lot of rough-and-tumble play. The girls played hard, too. The Kennedys' friends were also encouraged to play in the games. In fact, if they refused to play, they risked incurring Joe Kennedy

Even though his family's fortune was estimated at several million dollars, John F. Kennedy's boyhood allowance was 40 cents a week.

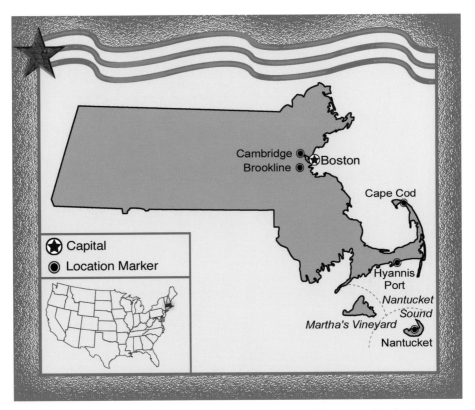

For most of the year, the Kennedys lived in Brookline, a suburb of Boston, but they spent summers at the family compound in Hyannis Port.

Sr.'s anger. Friends who wouldn't play touch football were often made to take their meals after the game in the kitchen.

The children's interest in the sea prompted their father to invest in larger and faster boats. One of the boats Joe Sr. bought was a 26-foot sailboat he gave Jack for his 15th birthday. Jack named her *Victura*, thinking the name had "something to do with winning." There was no question the *Victura* had everything to do with winning. The Kennedys joined the Wianno Yacht Club on Cape Cod. The children entered the club's races every weekend, winning so many silver cups that other children on the cape stopped entering, believing they had no

On Jack Kennedy's 15th birthday, his parents gave him a 26-foot-long sailboat. Jack named the vessel *Victura*. Throughout the rest of his life he sailed the craft whenever he had an opportunity. Dave Powers, a close friend, later commented, "the President . . . was never happier than when he was at the helm of *Victura*, sailing with family and friends." The sailboat is pictured here in front of the Kennedy Library in Massachusetts.

chance to beat the Kennedys. Later, Joe Kennedy bought a 22-foot sailboat in the "Star" class. The family named the boat *Flash II*. Star-class boats are the type of sailboats used by yacht racers in the Olympics as well as the America's Cup. When he was 19 years old, Jack Kennedy won two major races sailing the *Flash II*—becoming Nantucket Sound Star Class champion and then Atlantic Coast champion when he won a race staged along Long Island in New York.

At Harvard, there was no sailing team but there was a swim team. During his summers in Hyannis Port, Jack had loved swimming in Nantucket Sound. Joe and Rose Kennedy believed swimming was an excellent form of physical activity, and they insisted that all the Kennedy children learn to swim at an early age. Later, while serving in the Pacific Ocean during World War II, Jack would see his PT boat sliced apart by a Japanese ship, forcing him and the other crew members to swim for hours to a tiny island. Later, Jack spent a week swimming from island to island in search of a rescue party.

There was no question that he was a strong swimmer, but when he went out for the swim team at Harvard he once again found ill health getting in his way. Just before the team tryouts, Jack caught a severe cold and was sent to the campus infirmary.

Although weak with fever, Jack was determined to make the swim team. So he talked his friend Torby Macdonald into smuggling a thick steak and milk shake into the infirmary. Jack thought the heavy meal would build up his strength. He ate the meal, dressed, and sneaked out of the infirmary to take part in the trials.

When his race was called, Jack Kennedy was still running a fever. Still, he swam hard and just missed making the team. Torby watched the race from the deck of the pool.

"Guts is the word," Torby said. "He had plenty of guts."

The Muckers

George St. John, the *headmaster* of the Choate School, had a word for students who were lazy, paid little attention to their studies, and were constantly engaging in mischief. Such students, St. John liked to say, were "muckers."

Listening to that description as he entered Choate in 1930, Jack Kennedy resolved to become a mucker.

Jack Kennedy was probably the last new student Choate's headmaster suspected would be likely to get poor grades or display a love of mischief. Joe Jr. had already been to Choate, where he had been a top student and a leader of the school's sports teams. Once again, Jack found himself following his older brother, and once again he found himself in his older brother's shadow.

When Joe and Rose Kennedy moved into the Beals Street home in Brookline, they sent their children to the local public schools. But as Joe Sr. amassed his fortune, he could afford to send his children to the best and most expensive private

Jack Kennedy wears his best clothes for his confirmation in 1927. Confirmation is a ceremony that marks a transition to adulthood within the Roman Catholic Church.

schools. Choate, which is in Wallingford, Connecticut, was a boarding school, meaning that the children lived in dormitories on campus.

By the time he started Choate, Jack had already attended two other private schools. Although his teachers believed that he was highly intelligent, his grades had never been very good. Part of the problem was his health—he missed a lot of classes while recuperating from his many illnesses either at home or in the school infirmaries. In fact, at his second school, Canterbury School in New Milford, Connecticut, Jack seemed to be emerging from his shell and paying attention to his studies when he was suddenly hit with sharp pains near his stomach. The cause was his appendix, which had to be removed. He spent several weeks in the hospital recuperating from the surgery, and he never returned to Canterbury.

Because of Joe Jr.'s success at Choate, his parents had a great deal of respect for the school. They decided to send Jack there. At Choate, Jack struggled with his studies, had one of the messiest rooms in his *dormitory*, and failed to make the school's football team. But somehow he managed to stay healthy enough to settle in to a routine on campus. Soon after arriving on campus, Jack made two good friends: LeMoyne "Lem" Billings and Ralph "Rip" Horton. The three friends loved looking for trouble and avoiding their schoolwork as much as possible.

"Dear Dad," Jack wrote to his father, shortly after his grades were posted, "I thought I would write you right away as LeMoyne and I have been talking about how poorly we have done this quarter, and we have definitely decided to stop

During the 1930s Jack Kennedy attended the Choate School, an exclusive private boarding school; (inset) a photo of Kennedy from his Choate days.

any fooling around. . . . I really feel, now that I think it over, that I have been bluffing myself about how much real work I have been doing."

Joe Kennedy Sr. wrote back to his son, warning him to shape up. "Don't let me lose confidence in you again," he cautioned, "because it will be pretty nearly an impossible task to restore it—I am sure it will be a loss to you and a distinct loss to me. The mere trying to do a good job is not enough—real honest-to-goodness effort is what I expect."

The honest-to-goodness effort expected by Joe Kennedy Sr. wasn't about to happen anytime soon. In fact, Jack, Rip, and Lem took inspiration from their headmaster's warning about lazy and mischievous students, organizing what they called the "Muckers Club." They convinced about 10 other students to join. They bought little gold charms in the shape of a shovel that were inscribed with the letters "CMC," for Choate Muckers Club.

The Muckers had no other purpose than to find ways to break the rules. For example, after lights-out in the dormitories, the Muckers would gather together and sneak off campus for milk shakes at the local candy shop. Some of the Muckers sneaked cigarettes into their rooms. All of them seemed to ignore constant orders to clean up their rooms. They were always late for classes. During his last year at Choate, Jack was voted by his classmates as "Most Likely to Succeed," an honor reserved for Choate's most promising student. Later, the headmaster found out that Jack had rigged the election—promising favors to boys who agreed to vote for him.

JOHN FITZGERALD KENNEDY
Born May 29, 1917, in Brookline, Massachusetts. Prepared at The Choate School. Home Address: 294 Pondfield Road, Bronxville, New York. Winthrop House. *Crimson* (2–4); Chairman Smoker Committee (1); St. Paul's Catholic Club (1–4). Football (1), Junior Varsity (2); Swimming (1), Squad (2). Golf (1). House Hockey (3, 4); House Swimming (2); House Softball (4). Hasty Pudding-Institute of 1770; Spee Club. Permanent Class Committee. Field of Concentration: Government. Intended Vocation: Law.

This yearbook page shows the many clubs and activities Jack Kennedy was involved in at Harvard University. He graduated from the university in 1940—the year before the United States entered World War II.

Finally, St. John had had enough. He summoned Joe Kennedy Sr. to Choate.

Rip Horton recalled: "The Muckers thing was a serious affair. Why we weren't thrown out of school, I'll never know. I think the headmaster wanted to dismiss us all from school. He got up in chapel and publicly referred to us as bad apples in the basket. I think Jack was public enemy number one, Lem Billings was number two and I was number three."

Joe Kennedy Sr., Jack, and St. John met in the headmaster's office. St. John outlined all the problems with Jack—his laziness in class, his messy room, his leadership in the Muckers— and told Jack's father that the boy had to start shaping up or risk expulsion.

St. John recalled later, "At one point it came to the point where I was saying to myself, 'Well, I have two things to do, one to run the school, another to run Jack Kennedy and his friends.' They weren't bad, you know, but they had to be looked after. In other words, they weren't maturing. . . . Mr. Kennedy and Jack and I sat together, in my study, and I rehearsed the chapter and verse of things that had happened. And we said just what we thought, leaving nothing back, and Mr. Kennedy was supporting the school completely. I've always been very grateful to him."

During the meeting, St. John left Jack and his father alone in his study to answer a telephone call. Jack sat in the room, terrified at how his father would react to hearing about the trouble he had caused. But instead of showing anger, Joe Kennedy Sr. winked at his son. "You have the goods," he told Jack. "Why not try and show it?"

Camelot

Jack Kennedy graduated from Harvard University in 1940, just as hostilities in Europe and the Pacific Ocean made it clear the world would soon be plunged into war. In December 1941 the Japanese attacked Pearl Harbor. Jack had enlisted in the U.S. Navy four months before the attack. He soon took command of PT 109. In 1943, Kennedy heroically led his men in their fight to survive the wreck of their boat.

Following the war, he briefly found work as a news reporter but resigned to pursue a career in politics. Although his family hadn't lived in Boston in years, Jack moved back to the city so he could run for the U.S. House of Representatives in a neighborhood that had once been represented in Congress by his grandfather, Honey Fitz. It was a working-class area of the city—the residents were employed in factories or shops or held jobs in the building trades. Jack Kennedy, the son of a rich man, had to make the residents believe he could understand

John F. Kennedy relaxes with his wife, Jacqueline, and their children, Caroline and John. The glamour and energy of the Kennedys led many people to describe their time in the White House as "Camelot," after the mythical court of King Arthur.

their problems and represent their interests in Washington. He was given little chance to win the race, but Jack worked hard. He spent hours knocking on doors and introducing himself to the voters. When the votes were counted, he was declared the winner. At the age of 29, Jack Kennedy was on his way to Washington.

He won reelection to the House three times. In 1952 he successfully ran for the U.S. Senate.

That same year, he found himself confronted by a young, attractive newspaper photographer who wished to take his picture. Her name was Jacqueline Bouvier. The encounter soon led to a romance, and the two were married in 1953.

In Washington, John F. Kennedy was regarded as one of the bright young stars of the Democratic Party. But during the 1950s, the party was largely out of power. The president, Dwight D. Eisenhower, was a Republican. In 1956, Kennedy attempted to win the nomination of the Democratic Party to run for vice president alongside the party's presidential candidate, former Illinois governor Adlai E. Stevenson. Instead, party leaders turned to Senator Estes Kefauver of Tennessee. That fall, Stevenson and Kefauver lost to the Republican ticket, headed by Eisenhower and Vice President Richard M. Nixon.

More than 40,000 photographic negatives of John F. Kennedy and his family were destroyed during the terrorist attack on the World Trade Center in New York on September 11, 2001. The negatives were stored in a bank vault in the building by the family of the late Jacques Lowe, the Kennedys' longtime photographer.

As the 1960 election approached, it became clear to Democratic Party leaders that if they expected to capture the White House, they would need a young, vigorous candidate whose energy

> In 1957, Senator John F. Kennedy won a Pulitzer Prize for writing the book *Profiles in Courage*, which contained short biographies of American political heroes.

would electrify the campaign. They selected the young senator from Massachusetts.

The U.S. Constitution prohibits presidents from serving more than two consecutive terms, which meant Eisenhower was barred by law from running again in 1960. Vice President Nixon was selected by the Republican Party to head the ticket. In the fall of 1960, Nixon faced Kennedy in the presidential election.

Perhaps the most famous moment of the campaign occurred on September 26, when Kennedy and Nixon debated on live TV. Never before had a debate between presidential candidates been televised live to American voters. The Nixon-Kennedy debate featured many heated exchanges between the candidates on issues such as civil rights for African Americans and the growing threat to world peace of the former Soviet Union. Kennedy, at ease in front of the camera, projected confidence and warmth to the voters. Nixon, on the other hand, seemed nervous in front of the huge TV audience. Beads of sweat formed on his forehead, and, because of an oversight by a makeup artist, the vice president appeared to need a shave. Kennedy clearly scored well in the debate and won many votes that night.

Still, Kennedy was regarded as the underdog in the election. National politics had always been dominated by men of the Protestant faith, and the country had never before elected a Catholic to the presidency. But in the 1960 election, the voters showed they were ready to move beyond the old traditions. The nation cast its vote on November 8, and Kennedy was declared the winner by one of the thinnest margins in history. He was inaugurated in January 1961. At 43, he became the youngest elected president to take the oath of office.

As president, Kennedy set an agenda for America that he called the "New Frontier." America, he said, would use its might to guarantee freedom for oppressed people overseas. At the same time, he asked Americans to turn their attention on

John F. Kennedy sits in his rocking chair in the White House. Though Kennedy appeared to be strong and energetic, he suffered from many health problems and was often in pain.

their own society, to dedicate themselves to improving conditions at home.

"Ask not what your country can do for you," he said. "Ask what you can do for your country."

Americans were truly in love with their young president and his beautiful wife, who became known to millions of admirers simply as Jackie. She redecorated the White House, hosted gala parties in the Executive Mansion, and was admired by millions of American women for bringing style and glamour to Washington. Americans also loved the Kennedys' two little children: Caroline, born in 1957, and John Jr. (known as "John John"), who was born in 1960, just days after the election. The image of the young and attractive family occupying the White House reminded Americans of Camelot, the enchanted kingdom ruled by King Arthur. In fact, Camelot became a name many people used to refer to the Kennedy years in the White House.

President Kennedy made important decisions concerning civil rights. He sent federal marshals to all-white universities in Mississippi and Alabama to ensure that black students would be permitted to enroll.

In October 1962, U.S. Air Force spy planes photographed missile bases under construction on the island of Cuba. Cuba, which lies only 90 miles off the coast of Florida, was an ally of the Soviet Union, an enemy of the United States. President Kennedy and his advisers believed that the Soviets were placing, or were going to place, missiles with *nuclear warheads* on Cuba. If they were correct, the Soviet Union would be able to launch an attack that could destroy many of America's major

President Kennedy delivers a State of the Union address. Although Kennedy was assassinated before the end of his first term as president, programs he had started were eventually completed. These include civil rights legislation and landing American astronauts on the moon.

East Coast cities and kill millions of Americans—and the U.S. government would have only minutes of warning. Kennedy considered this too great a risk. He demanded that the Russians remove the missiles from Cuba. For 13 days, the United States and the Soviet Union teetered on the brink of war. Finally, Soviet leader Nikita Khrushchev backed down and ordered the missiles removed. Forcing the removal of the Soviet missiles from Cuba is regarded as Kennedy's greatest triumph.

Kennedy's presidency ended tragically on November 22, 1963. While riding in a motorcade in Dallas, Texas, the president was shot. He died a short time later in a local hospital. A government commission later concluded that the gunman was a young man named Lee Harvey Oswald and that he had acted alone in *assassinating* President Kennedy. Oswald himself was murdered two days later by a local nightclub owner, Jack Ruby.

Many people believe that the assassination of John F. Kennedy greatly changed the course of American history. For example, some people insist that Kennedy would have ended America's military involvement in Vietnam, sparing the country 10 years of a tragic and costly war.

We can only guess at what President Kennedy might have accomplished had he not been killed. But aside from thinking about what might have been, many Americans were affected on a personal level, too. Cut down in the prime of his life, the popular president left behind a young wife and two small children—and many Americans grieved as if the tragedy had happened in their own families. Photographers recorded many images that captured the nation's pain and grief in the days after the assassination. One especially sad and unforgettable image showed Jackie Kennedy, dressed all in black, with her children on the day of the funeral. As the flagged-draped coffin of his slain father passed by, three-year-old John Kennedy Jr. raised his hand to his forehead and saluted.

CHRONOLOGY

1849   Patrick Kennedy leaves Ireland and immigrates to Boston, Massachusetts.

1917   John F. Kennedy born on May 29 in Brookline, Massachusetts.

1928   Joseph and Rose Kennedy buy their summer home in Hyannis Port.

1930   John Kennedy enrolls at Choate School.

1936   Enrolls at Harvard University.

1941   Enlists in U.S. Navy.

1943   Leads his crew in surviving the wreck of their boat, PT 109.

1946   Wins first election to the U.S. House of Representatives from a working-class section of Boston.

1952   Wins election to the U.S. Senate.

1953   Marries Jacqueline Bouvier.

1956   Writes *Profiles in Courage*.

1957   Daughter Caroline born.

1960   Becomes youngest man ever elected president; son John Jr. born.

1962   Forces the Soviet Union to remove nuclear missiles from Cuba.

1963   Assassinated while riding in a motorcade in Dallas, Texas.

adobe—sun-dried mud used to make bricks.

appendix—a tube-like organ located near the stomach.

assassinate—to murder a prominent public figure, often the head of state.

calisthenics—exercises performed to enhance physical endurance.

cape—a piece of land that extends into a body of water.

cholera—an often-fatal disease marked by high fever and the inability of the sufferer to eat or retain fluids.

dormitory—a residence building for students at a college or private school.

financier—a person who provides money so that a business can operate; in return, the financier often receives some of the profits or a share in ownership of the business.

headmaster—the head of a private school, similar to a principal in a public school.

House of Representatives—the lower chamber of the U.S. Congress, composed of 435 representatives.

immigrant—a person who moves from one country to another for the purpose of establishing a permanent residence and becoming a citizen of the new country.

lampblack—soot from burned lamp oil.

mentally retarded—afflicted by a condition that prevents the brain from developing at a normal pace.

nuclear warhead—an extremely destructive bomb, made from a radioactive material such as plutonium, that is placed on a missile.

saloon—a place where alcoholic beverages are bought and consumed; a bar.

Senate—the upper chamber of the U.S. Congress, composed of 100 senators.

sound—a narrow passage of water between two landmasses.

torpedo—a bomb powered at sea by a self-contained engine.

varsity—the top team for a school in a given sport.

yacht—a large sailing boat, often used in races.

FURTHER READING

Anderson, Catherine Corley. *John F. Kennedy: Young People's President.* Minneapolis: Lerner Publications, 1991.

Kennedy, Rose Fitzgerald. *Times to Remember.* New York: Doubleday and Co., 1974.

Leamer, Laurence. *The Kennedy Men, 1901–1963.* New York: William Morrow & Co., 2001.

Livingstone, Harrison Edward, and Robert J. Groden. *High Treason: The Assassination of JFK and the Case for Conspiracy.* New York: Carroll and Graf, 1998.

McTaggart, Lynne. *Kathleen Kennedy: Her Life and Times.* New York: The Dial Press, 1983.

Mahoney, Richard D. *The Days of Jack and Bobby Kennedy.* New York: Arcade Publishing, 2000.

Perret, Geoffrey. *Jack: A Life Like No Other.* New York: Random House, 2001.

Randall, Marta. *John F. Kennedy.* Philadelphia: Chelsea House, 1988.

Reeves, Thomas C. *A Question of Character: A Life of John F. Kennedy.* New York: The Free Press, 1991.

INTERNET RESOURCES

- http://www.jfklibrary.org
    The John F. Kennedy Library

- http://www.whitehouse.gov/history/firstladies/jk35.html
    The White House Biography of Jacqueline Bouvier Kennedy

- http://www.whitehouse.gov/history/presidents/jk35.html
    The White House Biography of John F. Kennedy

INDEX

PICTURE CREDITS

3:   Photo. No. KFC 745N in the John F. Kennedy Library, Boston
8:   Photo. No. KFC 734N in the John F. Kennedy Library, Boston
11:   Photo. No. KFC 741N in the John F. Kennedy Library, Boston
12:   Courtesy the John F. Kennedy Library, Boston
14:   Photo. No. KFC 618N in the John F. Kennedy Library, Boston
17:   Courtesy the John F. Kennedy Library, Boston
18:   Photo. No. KFC 1128P in the John F. Kennedy Library, Boston
19:   Photo. No. 79Mus/FY-G in the John F. Kennedy Library, Boston
20:   Courtesy the John F. Kennedy Library, Boston

22:   Photo. No. KFC 214N in the John F. Kennedy Library, Boston
25:   © OTTN Publishing
26:   Photo. No. NLK91-C31:12A in the John F. Kennedy Library, Boston
28:   Photo. No. KFC 2183P in the John F. Kennedy Library, Boston
31:   both photographs courtesy of Choate Rosemary Hall
32:   Photo. No. 79Mus/FY-P30 in the John F. Kennedy Library, Boston
34:   Photo. No. ST-C22-1-62 in the John F. Kennedy Library, Boston
38:   Photo. No. KN-C20515 in the John F. Kennedy Library, Boston
40:   Photo. No. ST-C7-2-63 in the John F. Kennedy Library, Boston

Cover photos: all courtesy the John F. Kennedy Library, Boston (left, KFC 214N; center, ST-C237-1-63; right, KFC 2183P)

Contributors

ARTHUR M. SCHLESINGER JR. holds the Albert Schweitzer Chair in the Humanities at the Graduate Center of the City University of New York. He is the author of more than a dozen books, including *The Age of Jackson*; *The Vital Center*; *The Age of Roosevelt* (3 vols.); *A Thousand Days: John F. Kennedy in the White House*; *Robert Kennedy and His Times*; *The Cycles of American History*; and *The Imperial Presidency*. Professor Schlesinger served as Special Assistant to President Kennedy (1961–63). His numerous awards include the Pulitzer Prize for History; the Pulitzer Prize for Biography; two National Book Awards; the Bancroft Prize; and the American Academy of Arts and Letters Gold Medal for History.

HAL MARCOVITZ is a journalist for *The Morning Call*, a newspaper based in Allentown, Pennsylvania. He has written more than 30 books for young readers. He lives in Chalfont, Pennsylvania, with his wife, Gail, and daughters Ashley and Michelle.